FIVE LECTURES ON
PSYCHO-ANALYSIS

BY

SIGMUND FREUD

British Library Cataloguing-in-Publication Data
A catalogue record for this book is available from the
British Library

Contents

Five Lectures on Psycho-Analysis (1910)

By

Sigmund Freud

Delivered on the Occasion of the Celebration of the
Twentieth Anniversary of the Foundation of
CLARK UNIVERSITY, WORCESTER
MASSACHUSETTS
September 1909
To
DR. G. STANLEY HALL, PH.D., LL.D.
President of Clark University
Professor of Psychology and Pedagogics
This Work is Gratefully Dedicated

Sigmund Freud

Sigismund Schlomo Freud was born on 6th May 1856, in the Moravian town of Příbor, now part of the Czech Republic.

Sigmund was the eldest of eight children to Jewish Galician parents, Jacob and Amalia Freud. After Freud's father lost his business as a result of the Panic of 1857, the family were forced to move to Leipzig and then Vienna to avoid poverty. It was in Vienna that the nine-year-old Sigmund enrolled at the Leopoldstädter Kommunal-Realgymnasium before beginning his medical training at the University of Vienna in 1873, at the age of just 17. He studied a variety of subjects, including philosophy, physiology, and zoology, graduating with an MD in 1881.

The following year, Freud began his medical career in Theodor Meynert's psychiatric clinic at the Vienna General Hospital. He worked there until 1886 when he set up in private practice and began specialising in "nervous disorders". In the same year he married Merth Bernays, with whom he had 6 children between 1887 and 1895.

In the period between 1896 and 1901, Freud isolated himself from his colleagues and began work on developing the basics of his psychoanalytic theory. He published *The Interpretation of Dreams*, in 1899, to a lacklustre reception, but continued to produce works such as *The Psychopathology of Everyday Life* (1901) and *Three Essays on the Theory of Sexuality* (1905). He held a weekly meeting at his home known as the "Wednesday Psychological Society" which eventually developed into the Vienna Psycho-Analytic Society. His ideas gained momentum and by the end of the decade his methods were being used internationally by neurologists and psychiatrists.

Freud made a huge and lasting contribution to the field of psychology with many of his methods still being used in modern psychoanalysis. He inspired much discussion on the wealth of theories he produced and the reactions to his works began a century of great psychological investigation.

In 1930 Freud fled Vienna due to rise of Nazism and resided in England until his death from mouth cancer on 23rd September 1939.

FIRST LECTURE

LADIES AND GENTLEMEN, - It is with novel and bewildering feelings that I find myself in the New World, lecturing before an audience of expectant enquirers. No doubt I owe this honour only to the fact that my name is linked with the topic of psycho-analysis; and it is of psycho-analysis, therefore, that I intend to speak to you. I shall attempt to give you, as succinctly as possible, a survey of the history and subsequent development of this new method of examination and treatment.

If it is a merit to have brought psycho-analysis into being that merit is not mine.[1] I had no share in its earliest beginnings. I was a student and working for my final examinations at the time when another Viennese physician, Dr. Josef Breuer,[2] first (in 1880-2) made use of this procedure on a girl who was suffering from hysteria. Let us turn our attention straightaway to the history of this case and its treatment, which you will find set out in detail in the *Studies on Hysteria*[3] which were published later by Breuer and myself.

But I should like to make one preliminary remark. It is not without satisfaction that I have learnt that the majority of my audience are not members of the medical profession. You have no need to be afraid that any special medical knowledge will be required for following what I have to say. It is true that we shall go along with the doctors on the first stage of our journey, but we shall soon part company with them and, with Dr. Breuer, shall pursue a quite individual path.

1 [*Footnote added* 1923:] See, however, in this connection my remarks in 'A History of the Psycho-Analytic Movement' (1914*d*), where I assumed the entire responsibility for psycho-analysis.

2 Dr. Josef Breuer, born in 1842, a Corresponding Member of the Kaiserliche Akademie der Wissenschaften, is well known for his work on respiration and on the physiology of the sense of equilibrium.

3 Some of my contributions to this book have been translated into English by Dr. A. A. Brill of New York: *Selected Papers on Hysteria* (New York, 1909).

Dr. Breuer's patient was a girl of twenty-one, of high intellectual gifts. Her illness lasted for over two years, and in the course of it she developed a series of physical and psychological disturbances which decidedly deserved to be taken seriously. She suffered from a rigid paralysis, accompanied by loss of sensation, of both extremities on the right side of her body; and the same trouble from time to time affected her on her left side. Her eye movements were disturbed and her power of vision was subject to numerous restrictions. She had difficulties over the posture of her head;

she had a severe nervous cough. She had an aversion to taking nourishment, and on one occasion she was for several weeks unable to drink in spite of a tormenting thirst. Her powers of speech were reduced, even to the point of her being unable to speak or understand her native language. Finally, she was subject to conditions of '*absence*',[1] of confusion, of delirium, and of alteration of her whole personality, to which we shall have presently to turn our attention.

When you hear such an enumeration of symptoms, you will be inclined to think it safe to assume, even though you are not doctors, that what we have before us is a severe illness, probably affecting the brain, that it offers small prospect of recovery and will probably lead to the patient's early decease. You must be prepared to learn from the doctors, however, that, in a number of cases which display severe symptoms such as these, it is justifiable to take a different and a far more favourable view. If a picture of this kind is presented by a young patient of the female sex, whose vital internal organs (heart, kidneys, etc.) are shown on objective examination to be normal, but who has been subjected to violent *emotional* shocks - if, moreover, her various symptoms differ in certain matters of detail from what would have been expected - then doctors are not inclined to take the case too seriously. They decide that what they have before them is not an organic disease of the brain, but the enigmatic condition which, from the time of ancient Greek medicine, has been known as 'hysteria' and which has the power of producing illusory pictures of a whole number of serious diseases. They consider that there is then no risk to life but that a return to health - even a complete one - is probable. It is not always quite easy to distinguish a hysteria like this from a severe organic illness. There is no need for us to know, however, how a differential diagnosis of that kind is made; it will suffice to have an assurance that the case of Breuer's patient was precisely of a kind in which no competent physician could fail to make a diagnosis of hysteria. And here we may quote from the report of the patient's illness the further fact that it made its appearance at a time when she was nursing her father, of whom she was devotedly fond, through the grave illness which led to his death, and that, as a result of her own illness, she was obliged to give up nursing him.

¹ [The French term.]

So far it has been an advantage to us to accompany the doctors; but the moment of parting is at hand. For you must not suppose that a patient's prospects of medical assistance are improved in essentials by the fact that a diagnosis of hysteria has been substituted for one of severe organic disease of the brain. Medical skill is in most cases powerless against severe diseases of the brain; but neither can the doctor do anything against hysterical disorders. He must leave it to kindly Nature to decide when and how his optimistic prognosis shall be fulfilled.¹

Thus the recognition of the illness as hysteria makes little difference to the patient; but to the doctor quite the reverse. It is noticeable that his attitude towards hysterical patients is quite other than towards sufferers from organic diseases. He does not have the same sympathy for the former as for the latter: for the hysteric's ailment is in fact far less serious and yet it seems to claim to be regarded as equally so. And there is a further factor at work. Through his studies, the doctor has learnt many things that remain a sealed book to the layman: he has been able to form ideas on the causes of illness and on the changes it brings about - e.g. in the brain of a person suffering from apoplexy or from a malignant growth - ideas which must to some degree meet the case, since they allow him to understand the details of the illness. But all his knowledge - his training in anatomy, in physiology and in pathology - leaves him in the lurch when he is confronted by the details of hysterical phenomena. He cannot understand hysteria, and in the face of it he is himself a layman. This is not a pleasant situation for anyone who as a rule sets so much store by his knowledge. So it comes about that hysterical patients forfeit his sympathy. He regards them as people who are transgressing the laws of his science - like heretics in the eyes of the orthodox. He attributes every kind of wickedness to them, accuses them of exaggeration, of deliberate deceit, of malingering. And he punishes them by withdrawing his interest from them.

7

[1] I am aware that this is no longer the case; but in my lecture I am putting myself and my hearers back into the period before 1880. If things are different now, that is to a great extent the result of the activities whose history I am now sketching.

Dr. Breuer's attitude towards his patient deserved no such reproach. He gave her both sympathy and interest, even though, to begin with, he did not know how to help her. It seems likely that she herself made his task easier by the admirable qualities of intellect and character to which he has testified in her case history. Soon, moreover, his benevolent scrutiny showed him the means of bringing her a first instalment of help.

It was observed that, while the patient was in her states of '*absence* (altered personality accompanied by confusion), she was in the habit of muttering a few words to herself which seemed as though they arose from some train of thought that was occupying her mind. The doctor, after getting a report of these words, used to put her into a kind of hypnosis and then repeat them to her so as to induce her to use them as a starting point. The patient complied with the plan, and in this way reproduced in his presence the mental creations which had been occupying her mind during the '*absences*' and which had betrayed their existence by the fragmentary words which she had uttered. They were profoundly melancholy phantasies - 'day dreams' we should call them - sometimes characterized by poetic beauty, and their starting-point was as a rule the position of a girl at her father's sick-bed. When she had related a number of these phantasies, she was as if set free, and she was brought back to normal mental life. The improvement in her condition, which would last for several hours, would be succeeded next day by a further attack of '*absence*'; and this in turn would be removed in the same way by getting her to put into words her freshly constructed phantasies. It was impossible to escape the conclusion that the alteration in her mental state which was expressed in the '*absences*' was a result of the stimulus proceeding from these highly emotional phantasies. The patient herself, who, strange to say, could at this time only speak and understand English, christened this novel kind of treatment the 'talking cure'[1] or used to refer to it jokingly as 'chimney sweeping'.[1]

[1] [In English in the original.]

It soon emerged, as though by chance, that this process of sweeping the mind clean could accomplish more than the merely temporary relief of her ever-recurring mental confusion. It was actually possible to bring about the disappearance of the painful symptoms of her illness, if she could be brought to remember under hypnosis, with an accompanying expression of affect, on what occasion and in what connection the symptom had first appeared. 'It was in the summer during a period of extreme heat, and the patient was suffering very badly from thirst; for, without being able to account for it in any way, she suddenly found it impossible to drink. She would take up the glass of water that she longed for, but as soon as it touched her lips she would push it away like someone suffering from hydrophobia. As she did this, she was obviously in an *absence* for a couple of seconds. She lived only on fruit, such as melons, etc., so as to lessen her tormenting thirst. This had lasted for some six weeks, when one day during hypnosis she grumbled about her English "lady-companion", whom she did not care for, and went on to describe, with every sign of disgust, how she had once gone into this lady's room and how her little dog - horrid creature! - had drunk out of a glass there. The patient had said nothing, as she had wanted to be polite. After giving further energetic expression to the anger she had held back, she asked for something to drink, drank a large quantity of water without any difficulty, and awoke from her hypnosis with the glass at her lips; and thereupon the disturbance vanished, never to return.'[1]

With your permission, I should like to pause a moment over this event. Never before had anyone removed a hysterical symptom by such a method or had thus gained so deep an insight into its causation. It could not fail to prove a momentous discovery if the expectation were confirmed that others of the patient's symptoms - perhaps the majority of them - had arisen and could be removed in this same manner. Breuer spared no pains in convincing himself that this was so, and he proceeded to a systematic investigation of the pathogenesis of the other and more serious symptoms of the patient's illness. And it really *was* so. Almost all the symptoms had arisen in this way as residues - 'precipitates' they might be called - of emotional experiences. To these experiences, therefore, we later gave the name of 'psychical traumas', while the particular nature of the symptoms was explained by their relation to the traumatic scenes which were their cause. They were, to use a technical term, 'determined' by the scenes of whose recollection they represented residues, and it was no longer necessary to describe them as capricious or enigmatic products of the neurosis. One unexpected point, however, must be noticed. What left the symptom behind was not always a *single* experience. On the contrary, the result was usually brought about by the convergence of several traumas, and often by the repetition of a great number of similar ones. Thus it was necessary to reproduce the whole chain of pathogenic memories in chronological order, or rather in reversed order, the latest ones first and the earliest ones last; and it was quite impossible to jump over the later traumas in order to get back more quickly to the first, which was often the most potent one.

[1] *Studies on Hysteria.*

No doubt you will now ask me for some further instances of the causation of hysterical symptoms besides the one I have already given you of a fear of water produced by disgust at a dog drinking out of a glass. But if I am to keep to my programme I shall have to restrict myself to very few examples. In regard to the patient's disturbances of vision, for instance, Breuer describes how they were traced back to occasions such as one on which, 'when she was sitting by her father's bedside with tears in her eyes, he suddenly asked her what time it was. She could not see clearly; she made a great effort, and brought her watch near to her eyes. The face of the watch now seemed very big - thus accounting for her macropsia and convergent squint. Or again, she tried hard to suppress her tears so that the sick man should not see them.'[1] Moreover, all of the pathogenic impressions came from the period during which she was helping to nurse her sick father. 'She once woke up during the night in great anxiety about the patient, who was in a high fever; and she was under the strain of expecting the arrival of a surgeon from Vienna who was to operate. Her mother had gone away for a short time and Anna was sitting at the bedside with her right arm over the back of her chair. She fell into a waking dream and saw a black snake coming towards the sick man from the wall to bite him. (It is most likely that there were in fact snakes in the field behind the house and that these had previously given the girl a fright; they would thus have provided the material for her hallucination.) She tried to keep the snake off, but it was as though she was paralysed. Her right arm, over the back of the chair, had gone to sleep, and had become anaesthetic and paretic; and when she looked at it the fingers turned into little snakes with death's heads (the nails). (It seems probable that she had tried to use her paralysed right hand to drive off the snake and that its anaesthesia and paralysis has consequently become associated with the hallucination of the snake.) When the snake vanished, in her terror she tried to pray. But language failed her: she could find no tongue in which to speak, till at last she thought of some children's verses in English and then found herself able to think and pray in that language.'[1] When the patient had recollected this scene in hypnosis, the rigid paralysis of her left arm, which had persisted since the beginning of her illness, disappeared, and the treatment was brought to an end.

[1] *Studies on Hysteria.*

When, some years later, I began to employ Breuer's method of examination and treatment on patients of my own, my experiences agreed entirely with his. A lady, aged about forty, suffered from a *tic* consisting of a peculiar 'clacking' sound which she produced whenever she was excited, or sometimes for no visible reason. It had its origin in two experiences, whose common element lay in the fact that at the moment of their occurrence she had formed a determination not to make any noise, and in the fact that on both these occasions a kind of counter-will led her to break the silence with this same sound. On the first of these occasions one of her children had been ill, and, when she had at last with great difficulty succeeded in getting it off to sleep, she had said to herself that she must keep absolutely still so as not to wake it. On the other occasion, while she was driving with her two children in a thunderstorm, the horses had bolted and she had carefully tried to avoid making any noise for fear of frightening them even more.[1] I give you this one example out of a number of others which are reported in the *Studies on Hysteria*.[2]

[1] *Studies on Hysteria.*

[2] Extracts from that volume, together with some later writings of mine on hysteria, are now to be had in an English translation prepared by Dr. A. A. Brill of New York.

Ladies and Gentlemen, if I may be allowed to generalize - which is unavoidable in so condensed an account as this - I should like to formulate what we have learned so far as follows: *our hysterical patients suffer from reminiscences*. Their symptoms are residues and mnemic symbols of particular (traumatic) experiences. We may perhaps obtain a deeper understanding of this kind of symbolism if we compare them with other mnemic symbols in other fields. The monuments and memorials with which large cities are adorned are also mnemic symbols. If you take a walk through the streets of London, you will find, in front of one of the great railway termini, a richly carved Gothic column - Charing Cross. One of the old Plantagenet kings of the thirteenth century ordered the body of his beloved Queen Eleanor to be carried to Westminster; and at every stage at which the coffin rested he erected a Gothic cross. Charing Cross is the last of the monuments that commemorate the funeral cortège.[1] At another point in the same town, not far from London Bridge, you will find a towering, and more modern, column, which is simply known as 'The Monument'. It was designed as a memorial of the Great Fire, which broke out in that neighbourhood in 1666 and destroyed a large part of the city. These monuments, then, resemble hysterical symptoms in being mnemic symbols; up to that point the comparison seems justifiable. But what should we think of a Londoner who paused to-day in deep melancholy before the memorial of Queer Eleanor's funeral instead of going about his business in the hurry that modern working conditions demand or instead of feeling joy over the youthful queen of his own heart? Or again what should we think of a Londoner who shed tears before the Monument that commemorates the reduction of his beloved metropolis to ashes although it has long since risen again in far greater brilliance? Yet every single hysteric and neurotic behaves like these two unpractical Londoners. Not only do they remember painful experiences of the remote past, but they still cling to them emotionally; they cannot get free of the past and for its sake they neglect what is real and immediate. This fixation of mental life to pathogenic traumas is one of the most significant and practically important characteristics of neurosis.

I am quite ready to allow the justice of an objection that you are probably raising at this moment on the basis of the case history of Breuer's patient. It is quite true that all her traumas dated from the period when she was nursing her sick father and that her symptoms can only be regarded as mnemic signs of his illness and death. Thus they correspond to a display of mourning, and there is certainly nothing pathological in being fixated to the memory of a dead person so short a time after his decease; on the contrary, it would be a normal emotional process. I grant you that in the case of Breuer's patient there is nothing striking in her fixation to her trauma. But in other cases - such as that of the *tic* that I treated myself, where the determinants dated back more than fifteen and ten years - the feature of an abnormal attachment to the past is very clear; and it seems likely that Breuer's patient would have developed a similar feature if she had not received cathartic treatment so soon after experiencing the traumas and developing the symptoms.

[1] Or rather, it is a modern copy of one of these monuments. As Dr. Ernest Jones tells me, the name 'Charing' is believed to be derived from the words '*chère reine*'.

So far we have only been discussing the relations between a patient's hysterical symptoms and the events of her life. There are, however, two further factors in Breuer's observation which enable up to form some notion of how the processes of falling ill and of recovering occur.

In the first place, it must be emphasized that Breuer's patient, in almost all her pathogenic situations, was obliged to *suppress* a powerful emotion instead of allowing its discharge in the appropriate signs of emotion, words or actions. In the episode of her lady-companion's dog, she suppressed any manifestation of her very intense disgust, out of consideration for the woman's feelings; while she watched at her father's bedside she was constantly on the alert to prevent the sick man from observing her anxiety and her painful depression. When subsequently she reproduced these scenes in her doctor's presence the affect which had been inhibited at the time emerged with peculiar violence, as though it had been saved up for a long time. Indeed, the symptom which was left over from one of these scenes would reach its highest pitch of intensity at the time when its determining cause was being approached, only to vanish when that cause had been fully ventilated. On the other hand, it was found that no result was produced by the recollection of a scene in the doctor's presence if for some reason the recollection took place without any generation of affect. Thus it was what happened to these affects, which might be regarded as displaceable magnitudes, that was the decisive factor both for the onset of illness and for recovery. One was driven to assume that the illness occurred because the affects generated in the pathogenic situations had their normal outlet blocked, and that the essence of the illness lay in the fact that these 'strangulated' affects were then put to an abnormal use. In part they remained as a permanent burden upon the patient's mental life and a source of constant excitation for it; and in part they underwent a transformation into unusual somatic innervations and inhibitions, which manifested themselves as the physical symptoms of the case. For this latter process we coined the term 'hysterical conversion'. Quite apart from this, a certain portion of our mental excitation is normally directed along the paths of somatic innervation and produces what we know as an 'expression of the emotions'. Hysterical conversion exaggerates this portion of the discharge of an emotionally cathected mental process; it represents a far more intense expression of the emotions, which has entered upon a new path. When the bed of a stream is divided into two channels, then, if the current in one of them is brought up against an obstacle, the other will at once be overfilled. As you see, we are on the point of arriving at a purely psychological theory of hysteria, with affective processes in the front rank.

A second observation of Breuer's, again, compels us to attach great importance, among the characteristics of the pathological chain of events, to states of consciousness. Breuer's patient exhibited, alongside of her normal state, a number of mental peculiarities: conditions of '*absence*', confusion, and alterations of character. In her normal state she knew nothing of the pathogenic scenes or their connection with her symptoms; she had forgotten the scenes, or at all events had severed the pathogenic link. When she was put under hypnosis, it was possible, at the expense of a considerable amount of labour, to recall the scenes to her memory; and, through this work of recollecting, the symptoms were removed. The explanation of this fact would be a most awkward business, were it not that the way is pointed by experiences and experiments in hypnotism. The study of hypnotic phenomena has accustomed us to what was at first a bewildering realization that in one and the same individual there can be several mental groupings, which can remain more or less independent of one another, which can 'know nothing' of one another and which can alternate with one another in their hold upon consciousness. Cases of this kind, too, occasionally appear spontaneously, and are then described as examples of '*double conscience*'.[1] If, where a splitting of the personality such as this has occurred, consciousness remains attached regularly to one of the two states, we call it the *conscious* mental state and the other, which is detached from it, the *unconscious* one. In the familiar condition known as 'post-hypnotic suggestion', a command given under hypnosis is slavishly carried out subsequently in the normal state. This phenomenon affords an admirable example of the influences which the unconscious state can exercise over the conscious one; moreover, it provides a pattern upon which we can account for the phenomena of hysteria. Breuer adopted a hypothesis that hysterical symptoms arise in peculiar mental conditions to which he gave the name of 'hypnoid'. On this view, excitations occurring during these hypnoid states can easily become pathogenic because such states do not provide opportunities for the normal discharge of the process of excitation. There consequently arises from the process of excitation an unusual product - the symptom. This finds its way, like a foreign body, into the normal state, which in turn is in ignorance of the hypnoid pathogenic situation. Wherever there is a symptom there is also an amnesia, a gap in the memory, and filling up this gap implies the removal of the conditions which led to the production of the symptom.

[1] [The French term for 'dual consciousness'.]

This last part of my account will not, I fear, strike you as particularly clear. But you should bear in mind that we are dealing with novel and difficult considerations, and it may well be that it is not possible to make them much clearer - which shows that we still have a long way to go in our knowledge of the subject. Moreover, Breuer's theory of 'hypnoid states' turned out to be impeding and unnecessary, and it has been dropped by psycho-analysis to-day. Later on, you will at least have a hint of the influences and processes that were to be discovered behind the screen of hypnoid states erected by Breuer. You will have rightly formed the opinion, too, that Breuer's investigation has only succeeded in offering you a very incomplete theory and an unsatisfying explanation of the phenomena observed. But complete theories do not fall ready-made from the sky and you would have even better grounds for suspicion if anyone presented you with a flawless and complete theory at the very beginning of his observations. Such a theory could only be a child of his speculation and could not be the fruit of an unprejudiced examination of the facts.

SECOND LECTURE

LADIES AND GENTLEMEN, - At about the same time at which Breuer was carrying on the 'talking cure' with his patient, the great Charcot in Paris had begun the researches into hysterical patients at the Salpêtrière which were to lead to a new understanding of the disease. There was no possibility of his findings being known in Vienna at that time. But when, some ten years later, Breuer and I published our 'Preliminary Communication' on the psychical mechanism of hysterical phenomena, we were completely under the spell of Charcot's researches. We regarded the pathogenic experiences of our patients as psychical traumas, and equated them with the somatic traumas whose influence on hysterical paralyses had been established by Charcot; and Breuer's hypothesis of hypnoid states was itself nothing but a reflection of the fact that Charcot had reproduced those traumatic paralyses artificially under hypnosis.

The great French observer, whose pupil I became in 1885-6, was not himself inclined to adopt a psychological outlook. It was his pupil, Pierre Janet, who first attempted a deeper approach to the peculiar psychical processes present in hysteria, and we followed his example when we took the splitting of the mind and dissociation of the personality as the centre of our position. You will find in Janet a theory of hysteria which takes into account the prevailing views in France on the part played by heredity and degeneracy. According to him, hysteria is a form of degenerate modification of the nervous system, which shows itself in an innate weakness in the power of psychical synthesis. Hysterical patients, he believes, are inherently incapable of holding together the multiplicity of mental processes into a unity, and hence arises the tendency to mental dissociation. If I may be allowed to draw a homely but clear analogy, Janet's hysterical patient reminds one of a feeble woman who has gone out shopping and is now returning home laden with a multitude of parcels and boxes. She cannot contain the whole heap of them with her two arms and ten fingers. So first of all one object slips from her grasp; and when she stoops to pick it up, another one escapes her in its place, and so on. This supposed mental weakness of hysterical patients is not confirmed when we find that, alongside these phenomena of diminished capacity, examples are also to be observed of a partial increase in efficiency: as though by way of compensation. At the time when Breuer's patient had forgotten her mother tongue and every other language but English, her grasp of English reached such heights that, if she was handed a German book, she was able straight away to read out a correct and fluent translation of it.

When, later on, I set about continuing on my own account the investigations that had been begun by Breuer,

I soon arrived at another view of the origin of hysterical dissociation (the splitting of consciousness). A divergence of this kind, which was to be decisive for everything that followed, was inevitable, since I did not start out, like Janet, from laboratory experiments, but with therapeutic aims in mind.

I was driven forward above all by practical necessity. The cathartic procedure, as carried out by Breuer, presupposed putting the patient into a state of deep hypnosis; for it was only in a state of hypnosis that he attained a knowledge of the pathogenic connections which escaped him in his normal state. But I soon came to dislike hypnosis, for it was a temperamental and, one might almost say, a mystical ally. When I found that, in spite of all my efforts, I could not succeed in bringing more than a fraction of my patients into a hypnotic state, I determined to give up hypnosis and to make the cathartic procedure independent of it. Since I was not able at will to alter the mental state of the majority of my patients, I set about working with them in their *normal* state. At first, I must confess, this seemed a senseless and hopeless undertaking. I was set the task of learning from the patient something that I did not know and that he did not know himself. How could one hope to elicit it? But there came to my help a recollection of a most remarkable and instructive experiment which I had witnessed when I was with Bernheim at Nancy. Bernheim showed us that people whom he had put into a state of hypnotic somnambulism, and who had had all kinds of experiences while they were in that state, only *appeared* to have lost the memory of what they had experienced during somnambulism; it was possible to revive these memories in their normal state. It is true that, when he questioned them about their somnambulistic experiences, they began by maintaining that they knew nothing about them; but if he refused to give way, and insisted, and assured them that they *did* know about them, the forgotten experiences always reappeared.

So I did the same thing with my patients. When I reached a point with them at which they maintained that they knew nothing more, I assured them that they *did* know it all the same, and that they had only to say it; and I ventured to declare that the right memory would occur to them at the moment at which I laid my hand on their forehead. In that way I succeeded, without using hypnosis, in obtaining from the patients whatever was required for establishing the connection between the pathogenic scenes they had forgotten and the symptoms left over from those scenes. But it was a laborious procedure, and in the long run an exhausting one; and it was unsuited to serve as a permanent technique.

I did not abandon it, however, before the observations I made during my use of it afforded me decisive evidence. I found confirmation of the fact that the forgotten memories were not lost. They were in the patient's possession and were ready to emerge in association to what was still known by him; but there was some force that prevented them from becoming conscious and compelled them to remain unconscious. The existence of this force could be assumed with certainty, since one became aware of an effort corresponding to it if, in opposition to it, one tried to introduce the unconscious memories into the patient's consciousness. The force which was maintaining the pathological condition became apparent in the form of *resistance* on the part of the patient.

It was on this idea of resistance, then, that I based my view of the course of psychical events in hysteria. In order to effect a recovery, it had proved necessary to remove these resistances. Starting out from the mechanism of cure, it now became possible to construct quite definite ideas of the origin of the illness. The same forces which, in the form of resistance, were now offering opposition to the forgotten material's being made conscious, must formerly have brought about the forgetting and must have pushed the pathogenic experiences in question out of consciousness. I gave the name of '*repression*' to this hypothetical process, and I considered that it was proved by the undeniable existence of resistance.

The further question could then be raised as to what these forces were and what the determinants were of the repression in which we now recognized the pathogenic mechanism of hysteria. A comparative study of the pathogenic situations which we had come to know through the cathartic procedure made it possible to answer this question. All these experiences had involved the emergence of a wishful impulse which was in sharp contrast to the subject's other wishes and which proved incompatible with the ethical and aesthetic standards of his personality. There had been a short conflict, and the end of this internal struggle was that the idea which had appeared before consciousness as the vehicle of this irreconcilable wish fell a victim to repression, was pushed out of consciousness with all its attached memories, and was forgotten. Thus the incompatibility of the wish in question with the patient's ego was the motive for the repression; the subject's ethical and other standards were the repressing forces. An acceptance of the incompatible wishful impulse or a prolongation of the conflict would have produced a high degree of unpleasure; this unpleasure was avoided by means of repression, which was thus revealed as one of the devices serving to protect the mental personality.

To take the place of a number of instances, I will relate a single one of my cases, in which the determinants and advantages of repression are sufficiently evident. For my present purpose I shall have once again to abridge the case history and omit some important underlying material. The patient was a girl, who had lost her beloved father after she had taken a share in nursing him - a situation analogous to that of Breuer's patient. Soon afterwards her elder sister married, and her new brother-in-law aroused in her a peculiar feeling of sympathy which was easily masked under a disguise of family affection. Not long afterwards her sister fell ill and died, in the absence of the patient and her mother. They were summoned in all haste without being given any definite information of the tragic event. When the girl reached the bedside of her dead sister, there came to her for a brief moment an idea that might be expressed in these words: 'Now he is free and can marry me.' We may assume with certainty that this idea, which betrayed to her consciousness the intense love for her brother-in-law of which she had not herself been conscious, was surrendered to repression a moment later, owing to the revolt of her feelings. The girl fell ill with severe hysterical symptoms; and while she was under my treatment it turned out that she had completely forgotten the scene by her sister's bedside and the odious egoistic impulse that had emerged in her. She remembered it during the treatment and reproduced the pathogenic moment with signs of the most violent emotion, and, as a result of the treatment, she became healthy once more.

Perhaps I may give you a more vivid picture of repression and of its necessary relation to resistance, by a rough analogy derived from our actual situation at the present moment. Let us suppose that in this lecture-room and among this audience, whose exemplary quiet and attentiveness I cannot

28

sufficiently commend, there is nevertheless someone who is causing a disturbance and whose ill-mannered laughter, chattering and shuffling with his feet are distracting my attention from my task. I have to announce that I cannot proceed with my lecture; and thereupon three or four of you who are strong men stand up and, after a short struggle, put the interrupter outside the door. So now he is 'repressed', and I can continue my lecture. But in order that the interruption shall not be repeated, in case the individual who has been expelled should try to enter the room once more, the gentlemen who have put my will into effect place their chairs up against the door and thus establish a 'resistance' after the repression has been accomplished. If you will now translate the two localities concerned into psychical terms as the 'conscious' and the 'unconscious', you will have before you a fairly good picture of the process of repression.

You will now see in what it is that the difference lies between our view and Janet's. We do not derive the psychical splitting from an innate incapacity for synthesis on the part of the mental apparatus; we explain it dynamically, from the conflict of opposing mental forces and recognize it as the outcome of an active struggling on the part of the two psychical groupings against each other. But our view gives rise to a large number of fresh problems. Situations of mental conflict are, of course, exceedingly common; efforts by the ego to ward off painful memories are quite regularly to be observed without their producing the result of a mental split. The reflection cannot be escaped that further determinants must be present if the conflict is to lead to dissociation. I will also readily grant you that the hypothesis of repression leaves us not at the end but at the beginning of a psychological theory. We can only go forward step by step however, and complete knowledge must await the results of further and deeper researches.

Nor is it advisable to attempt to explain the case of Breuer's patient from the point of view of repression. That case history is not suited to this purpose, because its findings were reached with the help of hypnotic influence. It is only if you exclude hypnosis that you can observe resistances and repressions and form an adequate idea of the truly pathogenic course of events. Hypnosis conceals the resistance and renders a certain area of the mind accessible; but, as against this, it builds up the resistance at the frontiers of this area into a wall that makes everything beyond it inaccessible.

Our most valuable lesson from Breuer's observation was what it proved concerning the relation between symptoms and pathogenic experiences or psychical traumas, and we must not omit now to consider these discoveries from the standpoint of the theory of repression. At first sight it really seems impossible to trace a path from repression to the formation of symptoms. Instead of giving a complicated theoretical account, I will return here to the analogy which

I employed earlier for my explanation of repression. If you come to think of it, the removal of the interrupter and the posting of the guardians at the door may not mean the end of the story. It may very well be that the individual who has been expelled, and who has now become embittered and reckless, will cause us further trouble. It is true that he is no longer among us; we are free from his presence, from his insulting laughter and his *sotto voce* comments. But in some respects, nevertheless, the repression has been unsuccessful; for now he is making an intolerable exhibition of himself outside the room, and his shouting and banging on the door with his fists interfere with my lecture even more than his bad behaviour did before. In these circumstances we could not fail to be delighted if our respected president, Dr. Stanley Hall, should be willing to assume the role of mediator and peacemaker. He would have a talk with the unruly person outside and would then come to us with a request that he should be re-admitted after all: he himself would guarantee that the man would now behave better. On Dr. Hall's authority we decide to lift the repression, and peace and quiet are restored. This presents what is really no bad picture of the physician's task in the psycho-analytic treatment of the neuroses.

To put the matter more directly. The investigation of hysterical patients and of other neurotics leads us to the conclusion that their repression of the idea to which the intolerable wish is attached has been a *failure*. It is true that they have driven it out of consciousness and out of memory and have apparently saved themselves a large amount of unpleasure. *But the repressed wishful impulse continues to exist in the unconscious.* It is on the look-out for an opportunity of being activated, and when that happens it succeeds in sending into consciousness a disguised and unrecognizable *substitute* for what had been repressed, and to this there soon become attached the same feelings of unpleasure which it was hoped had been saved by the repression. This substitute for the repressed idea - the *symptom* - is proof against further attacks from the defensive ego; and in place of the short conflict an ailment now appears which is not brought to an end by the passage of time. Alongside the indication of distortion in the symptom, we can trace in it the remains of some kind of indirect resemblance to the idea that was originally repressed. The paths along which the substitution was effected can be traced in the course of the patient's psycho-analytic treatment; and in order to bring about recovery, the symptom must be led back along the same paths and once more turned into the repressed idea. If what was repressed is brought back again into conscious mental activity - a process which presupposes the overcoming of considerable resistances - the resulting psychical conflict, which the patient had tried to avoid, can, under the physician's guidance, reach a better outcome than was offered by repression. There are a number of such opportune solutions, which may bring the conflict and the neurosis to a happy end, and which may in certain instances be combined. The patient's personality may be convinced that it has been wrong in rejecting the pathogenic wish and may be led into accepting it wholly or in part; or the wish itself may be directed to a higher and consequently unobjectionable aim (this is what we call its 'sublimation'); or the rejection of the wish may be recognized as a justifiable one, but the automatic and therefore inefficient mechanism of repression may be replaced by a condemning judgement with the help of the highest human mental functions - conscious control of the wish is attained.

You must forgive me if I have not succeeded in giving you a more clearly intelligible account of these basic positions adopted by the method of treatment that is now described as 'psycho-analysis'. The difficulties have not lain only in the novelty of the subject. The nature of the incompatible wishes which, in spite of repression, succeed in making their existence in the unconscious perceptible, and the subjective and constitutional determinants which must be present in anyone before a failure of repression can occur and a substitute or symptom be formed - on all this I shall have more light to throw in some of my later observations.

THIRD LECTURE

LADIES AND GENTLEMEN, - It is not always easy to tell the truth especially when one has to be concise; and I am thus to-day obliged to correct a wrong statement that I made in my last lecture. I said to you that, having dispensed with hypnosis, I insisted on my patients nevertheless telling me what occurred to them in connection with the subject under discussion, and assured them that they really knew everything that they had ostensibly forgotten and that the idea that occurred to them would infallibly contain what we were in search of; and I went on to say to you that I found that the first idea occurring to my patients did in fact produce the right thing and turned out to be the forgotten continuation of the memory. This, however, is not in general the case, and I only put the matter so simply for the sake of brevity. Actually it was only for the first few times that the right thing which had been forgotten turned up as a result of simple insistence on my part. When the procedure we carried further, ideas kept on emerging that could not be the right ones, since they were not appropriate and were rejected as being wrong by the patients themselves. Insistence was of no further help at this point, and I found myself once more regretting my abandonment of hypnosis.

While I was thus at a loss, I clung to a prejudice the scientific justification for which was proved years later by my friend C. G. Jung and his pupils in Zurich. I am bound to say that it is sometimes most useful to have prejudices. I cherished a high opinion of the strictness with which mental processes are determined, and I found it impossible to believe that an idea produced by a patient while his attention was on the stretch could be an arbitrary one and unrelated to the idea we were in search of. The fact that the two ideas were not identical could be satisfactorily explained from the postulated psychological state of affairs. In the patient under treatment two forces were in operation against each other: on the one hand, his conscious endeavour to bring into consciousness the forgotten idea in his unconscious, and on the other hand, the resistance we already know about, which was striving to prevent what was repressed or its derivatives from thus becoming conscious. If this resistance amounted to little or nothing, what had been forgotten became conscious without distortion. It was accordingly plausible to suppose that the greater the resistance against what we were in search of becoming conscious, the greater would be its distortion. The idea which occurred to the patient in place of what we were in search of had thus itself originated like a symptom: it was a new, artificial and ephemeral substitute for what had been repressed, and was dissimilar to it in proportion to the degree of distortion it had undergone under the influence of the resistance. But, owing to its nature as a symptom, it must nevertheless have a certain similarity to what we were in search of; and if the resistance were not too great, we ought to be able to guess the latter from the former. The idea occurring to the patient must be in the nature of an *allusion* to the repressed element, like a representation of it in indirect speech.

We know cases in the field of normal mental life in which situations analogous to the one we have just assumed produce similar results. One such case is that of jokes. The problems of psycho-analytic technique have compelled me to investigate the technique of making jokes. I will give you one example of this - incidentally, a joke in English.

This is the anecdote.[1] Two not particularly scrupulous business men had succeeded, by dint of a series of highly risky enterprises, in amassing a large fortune, and they were now making efforts to push their way into good society. One method, which struck them as a likely one, was to have their portraits painted by the most celebrated and highly-paid artist in the city, whose pictures had an immense reputation. The precious canvases were shown for the first time at a large evening party, and the two hosts themselves led the most influential connoisseur and art critic up to the wall on which the portraits were hanging side by side. He studied the works for a long time, and then, shaking his head, as though there was something he had missed, pointed to the gap between the pictures and asked quietly: 'But where's the Saviour?'[2] I see you are all much amused at this joke. Let us now proceed to examine it. Clearly what the connoisseur meant to say was: 'You are a couple of rogues, like the two thieves between whom the Saviour was crucified.' But he did not say this. Instead he made a remark which seems at first sight strangely inappropriate and irrelevant, but which we recognize a moment later as an *allusion* to the insult that he had in mind and as a perfect substitute for it. We cannot expect to find in jokes *all* the characteristics that we have attributed to the ideas occurring to our patients, but we must stress the identity of the *motive* for the joke and for the idea. Why did the critic not tell the rogues straight out what he wanted to say? Because he had excellent counter-motives working against his desire to say it to their faces. There are risks attendant upon insulting people who are one's hosts and who have at their command the fists of a large domestic staff. One might easily meet with the fate which I suggested in my last lecture as an analogy for repression. That was the reason why the critic did not express the insult he had in mind directly but in the form of an 'allusion accompanied by omission'; and the same state of things is responsible for our patients' producing a more or less distorted *substitute* instead of the forgotten idea we are in search of.

[1] Cf. *Jokes and their Relation to the Unconscious*, 1905c.

[2] [In English in the original.]

It is highly convenient, Ladies and Gentlemen, to follow the Zurich school (Bleuler, Jung, etc.) in describing a group of interdependent ideational elements cathected with affect as a 'complex'. We see, then, that if in our search for a repressed complex in one of our patients we start out from the last thing he remembers, we shall have every prospect of discovering the complex, provided that the patient puts a sufficient number of his free associations at our disposal. Accordingly, we allow the patient to say whatever he likes, and hold fast to the postulate that nothing can occur to him which is not in an indirect fashion dependent on the complex we are in search of. If this method of discovering what is repressed strikes you as unduly circumstantial, I can at least assure you that it is the only practicable one.

When we come to putting this procedure into effect, we are subject to yet another interference. For the patient will often pause and come to a stop, and assert that he can think of nothing to say, and that nothing whatever occurs to his mind. If this were so and if the patient were right, then our procedure would once again have proved ineffective. But closer observation shows that such a stoppage of the flow of ideas never in fact occurs. It *appears* to happen only because the patient holds back or gets rid of the idea that he has become aware of, under the influence of the resistances which disguise themselves as various critical judgements about the value of the idea that has occurred to him. We can protect ourselves against this by warning him beforehand of this behaviour and requiring him to take no notice of such criticisms. He must, we tell him, entirely renounce any critical selection of this kind and say whatever comes into his head, even if he considers it incorrect or irrelevant or nonsensical, and above all if he finds it disagreeable to let himself think about what has occurred to him. So long as this ordinance is carried out we are certain of obtaining the material which will put us on the track of the repressed complexes.

This associative material, which the patient contemptuously rejects when he is under the influence of the resistance instead of under the doctor's, serves the psycho-analyst, as it were, as ore from which, with the help of some simple interpretative devices, he extracts its content of precious metal. If you are anxious to gain a rapid and provisional knowledge of a patient's repressed complexes, without as yet entering into their arrangement and interconnection, you will employ as a method of examination the 'association experiment' as it has been developed by Jung (1906) and his pupils. This procedure offers the psycho-analyst what qualitative analysis offers the chemist. In the treatment of neurotic patients it can be dispensed with; but it is indispensable for the objective demonstration of complexes and in the examination of the psychoses, which has been embarked on with so much success by the Zurich school.

Working over the ideas that occur to patients when they submit to the main rule of psycho-analysis is not our only technical method of discovering the unconscious. The same purpose is served by two other procedures: the interpretation of patients' dreams and the exploitation of their faulty and haphazard actions.

I must admit, Ladies and Gentlemen, that I hesitated for a long time whether, instead of giving you this condensed general survey of the whole field of psycho-analysis, it might not be better to present you with a detailed account of dream-interpretation.[1] I was held back by a purely subjective and seemingly secondary motive. It seemed to me almost indecent in a country which is devoted to practical aims to make my appearance as a 'dream-interpreter', before you could possibly know the importance that can attach to that antiquated and derided art. The interpretation of dreams is in fact the royal road to a knowledge of the unconscious; it is the securest foundation of psycho-analysis and the field in which every worker must acquire his convictions and seek(his training. If I am asked how one can become a psycho-analyst, I reply: 'By studying one's own dreams.' Every opponent of psycho-analysis hitherto has, with a nice discrimination, either evaded any consideration of *The Interpretation of Dreams*, or has sought to skirt over it with the most superficial objections. If, on the contrary, you can accept the solutions of the problems of dream-life, the novelties with, which psycho-analysis confronts your minds will offer you no further difficulties.

You should bear in mind that the dreams which we produce at night have, on the one hand, the greatest external similarity and internal kinship with the creations of insanity, and are, on the other hand, compatible with complete health in waking life. There is nothing paradoxical in the assertion that no one who regards these 'normal' illusions, delusions and character-changes with astonishment instead of comprehension has the slightest prospect of understanding the abnormal structures of pathological mental states otherwise than as a layman. You may comfortably count almost all psychiatrists among such laymen.

[1] *The Interpretation of Dreams* (1900*a*).

I invite you now to follow me on a brief excursion through the region of dream-problems. When we are awake we are in the habit of treating dreams with the same contempt with which patients regard the associations that are demanded of them by the psycho-analyst. We dismiss them, too, by forgetting them as a rule, quickly and completely. Our low opinion of them is based on the strange character even of those dreams that are not confused and meaningless, and on the obvious absurdity and nonsensicalness of other dreams. Our dismissal of them is related to the uninhibited shamelessness and immorality of the tendencies openly exhibited in some dreams. It is well known that the ancient world did not share this low opinion of dreams. Nor are the lower strata of our own society to-day in any doubt about the value of dreams; like the peoples of antiquity, they expect them to reveal the future. I confess that I feel no necessity for making any mystical assumptions in order to fill the gaps in our present knowledge, and accordingly I have never been able to find anything to confirm the prophetic nature of dreams. There are plenty of other things - sufficiently wonderful too - to be said about them.

In the first place, not all dreams are alien to the dreamer, incomprehensible and confused. If you inspect the dreams of very young children, from eighteen months upwards, you will find them perfectly simple and easy to explain. Small children always dream of the fulfilment of wishes that were aroused in them the day before but not satisfied. You will need no interpretative art in order to find this simple solution; all you need do is to enquire into the child's experiences on the previous day (the 'dream-day'). Certainly the most satisfactory solution of the riddle of dreams would be to find that adults' dreams too were like those of children - fulfilments of wishful impulses that had come to them on the dream-day. And such in fact is the case. The difficulties in the way of this solution can be overcome step by step if dreams are analysed more closely.

The first and most serious objection is that the content of adults' dreams is as a rule unintelligible and could not look more unlike the fulfilment of a wish. And here is the answer. Such dreams have been subjected to distortion; the psychical process underlying them might originally have been expressed in words quite differently. You must distinguish the *manifest content of the dream*, as you vaguely recollect it in the morning and laboriously (and, as it seems, arbitrarily) clothe it in words, and the *latent dream-thoughts*, which you must suppose were present in the unconscious. This distortion in dreams is the same process that you have already come to know in investigating the formation of hysterical symptoms. It indicates, too, that the same interplay of mental forces is at work in the formation of dreams as in that of symptoms. The manifest content of the dream is the distorted substitute for the unconscious dream-thoughts and this distortion is the work of the ego's forces of defence - of resistances. In waking life these resistances altogether prevent the repressed wishes of the unconscious from entering consciousness; and during the lowered state of sleep they are at least strong enough to oblige them to adopt a veil of disguise. Thereafter, the dreamer can no more understand the meaning of his dreams than the hysteric can understand the connection and significance of his symptoms.

You can convince yourself that there are such things as latent dream-thoughts and that the relation between them and the manifest content of the dream is really as I have described it, if you carry out an analysis of dreams, the technique of which is the same as that of psycho-analysis. You entirely disregard the apparent connections between the elements in the manifest dream and collect the ideas that occur to you in connection with each separate element of the dream by free association according to the psycho-analytic rule of procedure. From this material you arrive at the latent dream-thoughts, just as you arrived at the patient's hidden complexes from his associations to his symptoms and memories. The latent dream-thoughts which have been reached in this way will at once show you how completely justified we have been in tracing back adults' dreams to children's dreams. The true meaning of the dream, which has now taken the place of its manifest content, is always clearly intelligible; it has its starting-point in experiences of the previous day, and proves to be a fulfilment of unsatisfied wishes. The manifest dream, which you know from your memory when you wake up, can therefore only be described as a *disguised* fulfilment of *repressed* wishes.

You can also obtain a view, by a kind of synthetic work, of the process which has brought about the distortion of the unconscious dream-thoughts into the manifest content of the dream. We call this process the 'dream-work'. It deserves our closest theoretical interest, since we are able to study in it, as nowhere else, what unsuspected psychical processes can occur in the unconscious, or rather, to put it more accurately, *between* two separate psychical systems like the conscious and unconscious. Among these freshly discovered psychical processes those of *condensation* and *displacement* are especially noticeable. The dream-work is a special case of the effects produced by two different mental groupings on each other - that is, of the consequences of mental splitting; and it seems identical in all essentials with the process of distortion which transforms the repressed complexes into symptoms where there is unsuccessful repression.

You will also learn with astonishment from the analysis of dreams (and most convincingly from that of your own) what an unsuspectedly great part is played in human development by impressions and experiences of early childhood. In dream-life the child that is in man pursues its existence, as it were, and retains all its characteristics and wishful impulses, even such as have become unserviceable in later life. There will be brought home to you with irresistible force the many developments, repressions, sublimations and reaction-formations, by means of which a child with a quite other innate endowment grows into what we call a normal man, the bearer, and in part the victim, of the civilization that has been so painfully acquired.

I should like you to notice, too, that the analysis of dreams has shown us that the unconscious makes use of a particular symbolism, especially for representing sexual complexes. This symbolism varies partly from individual to individual; but partly it is laid down in a typical form and seems to coincide with the symbolism which, as we suspect, underlies our myths and fairy tales. It seems not impossible that these creations of the popular mind might find an explanation through the help of dreams.

Lastly, I must warn you not to let yourselves be put out by the objection that the occurrence of anxiety-dreams contradicts our view of dreams as the fulfilments of wishes. Apart from the fact that these anxiety-dreams, like the rest, require interpretation before any judgement can be formed on them, it must be stated quite generally that the anxiety does not depend on the content of the dream in such a simple manner as one might imagine without having more knowledge and taking more account of the determinants of neurotic anxiety. Anxiety is one of the ego's reactions in repudiation of repressed wishes that have become powerful; and its occurrence in dreams as well is very easily explicable when the formation of the dream has been carried out with too much of an eye to the fulfilment of these repressed wishes.

As you see, research into dreams would be justified for its own sake merely by the information it gives us on matters that can with difficulty be discovered in other ways. But we were in fact led to the subject in connection with the psycho-analytic treatment of neurotics. You will easily understand from what I have already said how it is that dream-interpretation, if it is not made too difficult by the patient's resistances, leads to a knowledge of his hidden and repressed wishes and of the complexes nourished by them; and I can now pass on to the third group of mental phenomena whose study has become one of the technical instruments of psycho-analysis.

The phenomena in question are the small faulty actions performed by both normal and neurotic people, to which as a rule no importance is attached: forgetting things that might be known and sometimes in fact

are known (e.g. the occasional difficulty in recalling proper names), slips of the tongue in talking, by which we ourselves are so often affected, analogous slips of the pen and misreadings, bungling the performance of actions, losing objects or breaking them. All of these are things for which as a rule no psychological determinants are sought and which are allowed to pass without criticism as consequences of distraction or inattention or similar causes. Besides these there are the actions and gestures which people carry out without noticing them at all, to say nothing of attributing any psychological importance to them: playing about and fiddling with things, humming tunes, fingering parts of one's own body or one's clothing and so on.[1] These small things, faulty actions and symptomatic or haphazard actions alike, are not so insignificant as people, by a sort of conspiracy of silence, are ready to suppose. They always have a meaning, which can usually be interpreted with ease and certainty from the situation in which they occur. And it turns out that once again they give expression to impulses and intentions which have to be kept back and hidden from one's own consciousness, or that they are actually derived from the same repressed wishful impulses and complexes which we have already come to know as the creators of symptoms and the constructors of dreams. They therefore deserve to be rated as symptoms, and if they are examined they may lead, just as dreams do, to the uncovering of the hidden part of the mind. A man's most intimate secrets are as a rule betrayed by their help. If they occur particularly easily and frequently even in healthy people in whom the repression of unconscious impulses has on the whole been quite successful, they have their triviality and inconspicuousness to thank for it. But they can claim a high theoretical value, since they prove that repression and the formation of substitutes occur even under healthy conditions.

[1] Cf. *The Psychopathology of Everyday Life* (1901*b*).

As you already see, psycho-analysts are marked by a particularly strict belief in the determination of mental life. For them there is nothing trivial, nothing arbitrary or haphazard. They expect in every case to find sufficient motives where, as a rule, no such expectation is raised. Indeed, they are prepared to find *several* motives for one and the same mental occurrence, whereas what seems to be our innate craving for causality declares itself satisfied with a *single* psychical cause.

If you will now bring together the means we possess for uncovering what is concealed, forgotten and repressed in the mind (the study of the ideas occurring to patients under free association, of their dreams and of their faulty and symptomatic actions), and if you will add to these the exploitation of certain other phenomena which occur during psycho-analytic treatment and on which I shall have a few remarks to make later under the heading of 'transference' - if you bear all these in mind, you will agree with me in concluding that our technique is already efficient enough to fulfil its task, to bring the pathogenic psychical material into consciousness and so to get rid of the ailments that have been brought about by the formation of substitutive symptoms. And if, in the course of our therapeutic endeavours, we extend and deepen our knowledge of the human mind both in health and sickness, that can, of course, only be regarded as a peculiar attraction in our work.

You may have formed an impression that the technique through whose armoury I have just conducted you is particularly difficult. In my opinion that technique is entirely in conformity with the material with which it has to deal. But this much at least is clear: it is not a self-evident one and it must be learnt just as the techniques of histology or surgery must be learnt. You will perhaps be surprised to hear that in Europe we have heard a large number of judgements on psycho-analysis from people who know nothing of this technique and do not employ it; and who go on to demand with apparent scorn that we shall prove to them the correctness of our findings. Among these adversaries there are no doubt some to whom a scientific mode of thought is not as a rule alien, who, for instance, would not reject the results of a microscopic examination because it could not be confirmed on the anatomical preparation with the naked eye, but who would first form a judgement on the matter themselves with the help of a microscope. But, where psycho-analysis is concerned, the prospects of recognition are in truth less favourable. Psycho-analysis is seeking to bring to conscious recognition the things in mental life which are repressed; and everyone who forms a judgement on it is himself a human being, who possesses similar repressions and may perhaps be maintaining them with difficulty. They are therefore bound to call up the same resistance in him as in our patients; and that resistance finds it easy to disguise itself is an intellectual rejection and to bring up arguments like those which we ward off in our patients by means of the fundamental rule of psycho-analysis. We often become aware in our opponents, just as we do in our patients, that their power of judgement is very noticeably influenced affectively in the sense of being diminished. The arrogance of consciousness (in rejecting dreams with such contempt, for instance) is one of the most powerful of the devices with which we are provided as a universal protection against the incursion of unconscious complexes. That is why it is so hard to convince people of the reality of the unconscious and to teach them to recognize something new which is in contradiction to their conscious knowledge.

FOURTH LECTURE

LADIES AND GENTLEMEN, - You will want to know now what we have found out about the pathogenic complexes and repressed wishful impulses of neurotics with the help of the technical methods I have described.

First and foremost we have found out one thing. Psychoanalytic research traces back the symptoms of patients' illnesses with really surprising regularity to impressions from their *erotic life*. It shows us that the pathogenic wishful impulses are in the nature of erotic instinctual components; and it forces us to suppose that among the influences leading to the illness the predominant significance must be assigned to erotic disturbances, and that this is the case in both sexes.

I am aware that this assertion of mine will not be willingly believed. Even workers who are ready to follow my psychological studies are inclined to think that I overestimate the part played by sexual factors; they meet me with the question why *other* mental excitations should not lead to the phenomena I have described of repression and the formation of substitutes. I can only answer that I do not know why they should not, and that I should have no objection to their doing so; but experience shows that they do not carry this weight, that at most they *support* the operation of the sexual factors but cannot replace them. Far from this position having been postulated by me theoretically, at the time of the joint publication of the *Studies* with Dr. Breuer in 1895 I had not yet adopted it; and I was only converted to it when my experiences became more numerous and penetrated into the subject more deeply. There are among my present audience a few of my closest friends and followers, who have travelled with me here to Worcester. Enquire from them, and you will hear that they all began by completely disbelieving my assertion that sexual aetiology was of decisive importance, until their own analytic experiences compelled them to accept it.

A conviction of the correctness of this thesis was not precisely made easier by the behaviour of patients. Instead of willingly presenting us with information about their sexual life, they try to conceal it by every means in their power. People are in general not candid over sexual matters. They do not show their sexuality freely, but to conceal it they wear a heavy overcoat woven of a tissue of lies, as though the weather were bad in the world of sexuality. Nor are they mistaken. It is a fact that sun and wind are not favourable to sexual activity in this civilized world of ours; none of us can reveal his erotism freely to others. But when your patients discover that they can feel quite easy about it while they are under your treatment, they discard this veil of lies, and only then are you in a position to form a judgement on this debatable question. Unluckily even doctors are not preferred above other human creatures in their personal relation to questions of sexual life, and many of them are under the spell of the combination of prudery and prurience which governs the attitude of most 'civilized people' in matters of sexuality.

Let me now proceed with my account of our findings. In another set of cases psycho-analytic investigation traces the symptoms back, it is true, not to sexual experiences but to commonplace traumatic ones. But this distinction loses its significance owing to another circumstance. For the work of analysis required for the thorough explanation and complete recovery of a case never comes to a stop at events that occurred at the time of the onset of the illness, but invariably goes back to the patient's puberty and early childhood; and it is only there that it comes upon the impressions and events which determined the later onset of the illness. It is only experiences in childhood that explain susceptibility to later traumas and it is only by uncovering these almost invariably forgotten memory-traces and by making them conscious that we acquire the power to get rid of the symptoms. And here we reach the same conclusion as in our investigation of dreams: the imperishable, repressed wishful impulses of childhood have alone provided the power for the construction of symptoms, and without them the reaction to later traumas would have taken a normal course. But these powerful wishful impulses of childhood may without exception be described as sexual.

And now at last I am quite certain that I have surprised you. 'Is there such a thing, then, as infantile sexuality?' you will ask 'Is not childhood on the contrary the period of life that is marked by the absence of the sexual instinct?' No, Gentlemen, it is certainly not the case that the sexual instinct enters into children at the age of puberty in the way in which, in the Gospel, the devil entered into the swine. A child has its sexual instincts and activities from the first; it comes into the world with them; and, after an important course of development passing through many stages, they lead to what is known as the normal sexuality of the adult. There is even no difficulty in observing the manifestations of these sexual activities in children; on the contrary, it calls for some skill to overlook them or explain them away.

By a lucky chance I am in a position to call a witness in favour of my assertions from your very midst. I have here in my hand a paper written by a Dr. Sanford Bell, which was published in *The American Journal of Psychology* in 1902. The author is a Fellow of Clark University, of the very institution in whose lecture-room we are now assembled. In this work, which is entitled 'A Preliminary Study of the Emotion of Love between the Sexes', and which appeared three years before my *Three Essays on the Theory of Sexuality*, the author says exactly what I have just told you: 'The emotion of sex-love . . . does not make its appearance for the first time at the period of adolescence, as has been thought.' He carried out his work in what we in Europe would call 'the American manner', collecting no fewer than 2,500 positive observations in the course of fifteen years, among them 800 of his own. Concerning the signs by which these instances of falling in love are revealed he writes as follows: 'The unprejudiced mind in observing these manifestations in hundreds of couples of children cannot escape referring them to sex origin. The most exacting mind is satisfied when to these observations are added the confessions of those who have, as children, experienced the emotion to a marked degree of intensity and whose memories of childhood are relatively distinct.' But those of you who do not wish to believe in infantile sexuality will be most of all surprised to hear that not a few of these children who have fallen in love so early are of the tender age of three, four and five.

It would not astonish me if you were to attach more credence to these observations made by one of your closest neighbours than to mine. I myself have recently been fortunate enough to obtain a fairly complete picture of the somatic instinctual manifestations and mental products at an early stage of a child's erotic life from the analysis of a five-year-old boy, suffering from anxiety - an analysis carried out with a correct technique by his own father.[1] And I may remind you that only a few hours ago, in this same room, my friend Dr. C. G. Jung reported an observation to you made on a still younger girl who, with a precipitating cause similar to my patient's (the birth of a younger child in the family), made it possible to infer with certainty the presence of almost the same sensual impulses, wishes and complexes. I do not despair, therefore, of your becoming reconciled to what seems at first sight the strange idea of infantile sexuality. And I should like to quote to you the praiseworthy example of the Zurich psychiatrist, Dr. E. Bleuler, who declared publicly not many years ago that he was 'unable to comprehend my theories of sexuality', and who has since then confirmed the existence of infantile sexuality to its full extent from his own observations. (Cf. Bleuler, 1908.)

It is only too easy to explain why most people (whether medical observers or others) will hear nothing of the sexual life of children. They have forgotten their own infantile sexual activity under the pressure of their education to a civilized life, and they do not wish to be reminded of what has been repressed. They would arrive at other convictions if they were to begin their enquiry with a self-analysis, a revision and interpretation of their childhood memories.

[1] 'The Analysis of a Phobia in a Five-Year-Old Boy'.

Put away your doubts, then, and join me in a consideration of infantile sexuality from the earliest age.[1] A child's sexual instinct turns out to be put together out of a number of factors; it is capable of being divided up into numerous components which originate from various sources. Above all, it is still independent of the reproductive function, into the service of which it will later be brought. It serves for the acquisition of different kinds of pleasurable feeling, which, basing ourselves on analogies and connections, we bring together under the idea of sexual pleasure. The chief source of infantile sexual pleasure is the appropriate excitation of certain parts of the body that are especially susceptible to stimulus: apart from the genitals, these are the oral, anal and urethral orifices, as well as the skin and other sensory surfaces. Since at this first phase of infantile sexual life satisfaction is obtained from the subject's own body and extraneous objects are disregarded, we term this phase (from a word coined by Havelock Ellis) that of *auto-erotism*. We call the parts of the body that are important in the acquisition of sexual pleasure 'erotogenic zones'. Thumb-sucking (or sensual sucking) in the youngest infants is a good example of this auto-erotic satisfaction from an erotogenic zone. The first scientific observer of this phenomenon, a paediatrician in Budapest named Lindner (1879), already interpreted it correctly as sexual satisfaction and described exhaustively its transition to other and higher forms of sexual activity. Another sexual satisfaction at this period of life is the masturbatory excitation of the genitals, which retains so much importance in later life and by many people is never completely conquered. Alongside these and other auto-erotic activities, we find in children at a very early age manifestations of those instinctual components of sexual pleasure (or, as we like to say, of libido) which presuppose the taking of an extraneous person as an object. These instincts occur in pairs of opposites, active and passive. I may mention as the most important representatives of this group the desire to cause pain (sadism) with its passive counterpart (masochism) and the active and passive desire for looking, from the former of which curiosity branches off later on and from the latter the impulsion to artistic and theatrical display. Others of a child's sexual activities already imply the making of an 'object-choice', where an extraneous person becomes the main feature, a person who owes his importance in the first instance to considerations arising from the self-preservative instinct. But at this early period of childhood difference in sex plays no decisive part as yet. Thus you can attribute some degree of homosexuality to every child without doing him an injustice. This widespread and copious but dissociated sexual life of children, in which each separate instinct pursues its own acquisition of pleasure independently of all the rest, is now brought together and organized in two main directions, so that by the end of puberty the individual's final sexual character is as a rule completely formed. On the one hand, the separate instincts become subordinated to the dominance of the genital zone, so that the whole sexual life enters the service of reproduction, and the satisfaction of the separate instincts retains its importance only as preparing for and encouraging the sexual act proper. On the other hand, object-choice pushes auto-erotism into the background, so that in the subject's erotic life all the components of the sexual instinct now seek satisfaction in relation to the person who is loved. Not all of the original sexual components, however, are admitted to take part in this final establishment of sexuality. Even before puberty extremely energetic repressions of certain instincts have been effected under the influence of education, and mental forces such as shame, disgust and morality have been set up, which, like watchmen, maintain these repressions. So that when at puberty the high tide of sexual demands is reached, it is met by these mental reactive or resistant structures like dams, which direct its flow into what are called normal channels and make it impossible for it to reactivate the instincts that have undergone repression. It is in particular the coprophilic impulses of childhood - that is to say, the desires attaching to the excreta - which are submitted the most rigorously to repression, and the same is true, furthermore, of fixation to the figures to which the child's original object-choice was attached.

[1] Cf. *Three Essays on the Theory of Sexuality* (1905d).

There is a dictum in general pathology, Gentlemen, which asserts that every developmental process carries with it the seed of a pathological disposition, in so far as that process may be inhibited, delayed, or may run its course incompletely. The same thing is true of the highly complicated development of the sexual function. It does not occur smoothly in every individual; and, if not, it leaves behind it either abnormalities or a predisposition to fall ill later, along the path of involution (i.e. regression). It may happen that not all the component instincts submit to the dominance of the genital zone. An instinct which remains in this way independent leads to what we describe as a *perversion*, and may substitute its own sexual aim for the normal one. It very often happens, as I have already said, that auto-erotism is not completely conquered, and evidence of this is given by a great variety of subsequent disturbances. The originally equal value attached to the two sexes as sexual objects may persist, and this will lead to a tendency in adult life to homosexual activity, which can in certain circumstances be intensified into exclusive homosexuality. These classes of disturbance represent direct inhibitions in the development of the sexual function; they comprise the perversions and, what is by no means rare, general infantilism in sexual life.

The predisposition to *neurosis* is traceable to impaired sexual development in a different way. Neuroses are related to perversions as negative to positive. The same instinctual components as in the perversions can be observed in the neuroses as vehicles of complexes and constructors of symptoms, but in the latter case they operate from the unconscious. Thus they have undergone repression, but have been able, in defiance of it, to persist in the unconscious. Psycho-analysis makes it clear that an excessively strong manifestation of these instincts at a very early age leads to a kind of partial *fixation*, which then constitutes a weak point in the structure of the sexual function. If in maturity the performance of the normal sexual function comes up against obstacles, the repression that took place during the course of development will be broken through at the precise points at which the infantile fixations occurred.

But here you will perhaps protest that all this is not sexuality. I have been using the word in a far wider sense than that in which you have been accustomed to understand it. So much I am quite ready to grant you. But the question arises whether it is not rather you who have been using the word in far too narrow a sense by restricting it to the sphere of reproduction. It means that you are sacrificing an understanding of the perversions and the connection between the perversions, the neuroses and normal sexual life; and you are making it impossible for you to recognize in its true significance the easily observable beginnings of the somatic and mental erotic life of children. But however you may choose to decide the verbal usage, you should bear firmly in mind that psycho-analysts understand sexuality in the full sense to which one is led by a consideration of infantile sexuality.

Let us return to the sexual development of children. We have some arrears to make up owing to our having paid more attention to the somatic than to the mental phenomena of sexual life. The child's first choice of an object, which derives from its need for help, claims our further interest. Its choice is directed in the first instance to all those who look after it, but these soon give place to its parents. Children's relations to their parents, as we learn alike from direct observations of children and from later analytic examination of adults, are by no means free from elements of accompanying sexual excitation. The child takes both of its parents, and more particularly one of them, as the object of its erotic wishes. In so doing, it usually follows some indication from its parents, whose affection bears the clearest characteristics of a sexual activity, even though of one that is inhibited in its aims. As a rule a father prefers his daughter and a mother her son; the child reacts to this by wishing, if he is a son, to take his father's place, and, if she is a daughter, her mother's. The feelings which are aroused in these relations between parents and children and in the resulting ones between brothers and sisters are not only of a positive or affectionate kind but also of a negative or hostile one. The complex which is thus formed is doomed to early repression; but it continues to exercise a great and lasting influence from the unconscious. It is to be suspected that, together with its extensions, it constitutes the *nuclear complex* of every neurosis, and we may expect to find it no less actively at work in other regions of mental life. The myth of King Oedipus, who killed his father and took his mother to wife, reveals, with little modification, the infantile wish, which is later opposed and repudiated by the *barrier against incest*. Shakespeare's *Hamlet* is equally rooted in the soil of the incest-complex, but under a better disguise.

During the time when the child is dominated by the still unrepressed nuclear complex, an important part of his intellectual activity is brought into the service of his sexual interests. He begins to enquire where babies come from, and, on the basis of the evidence presented to him, guesses more of the true facts than the grown-ups imagine. His interest in these researches is usually set going by the very real threat offered to him by the arrival of a new baby, which to begin with he regards merely as a competitor. Under the influence of the component instincts that are active in himself, he arrives at a number of 'infantile sexual theories' - such as attributing a male genital organ to both sexes alike, or supposing that babies are conceived by eating and born through the end of the bowel, or regarding sexual intercourse as a hostile act, a kind of violent subjugation. But as a result precisely of the incompleteness of his sexual constitution, and of the gap in his knowledge due to the hidden nature of the female sexual channel, the young investigator is obliged to abandon his work as a failure. The fact of this childish research itself, as well as the different infantile sexual theories that it brings to light, remain of importance in determining the formation of the child's character and the content of any later neurotic illness.

It is inevitable and perfectly normal that a child should take his parents as the first objects of his love. But his libido should not remain fixated to these first objects; later on, it should merely take them as a model, and should make a gradual transition from them on to extraneous people when the time for the final choice of an object arrives. The detachment of the child from his parents is thus a task that cannot be evaded if the young individual's social fitness is not to be endangered. During the time at which repression is making its selection among the component instincts, and later, when there should be a slackening of the parents' influence, which is essentially responsible for the expenditure of energy on these repressions, the task of education meets with great problems, which at the present time are certainly not always dealt with in an understanding and unobjectionable manner.

You must not suppose, Ladies and Gentlemen, that these discussions on sexual life and the psychosexual development of children have led us too far from psycho-analysis and the problem of curing nervous disorders. You can, if you like, regard psycho-analytic treatment as no more than a prolongation of education for the purpose of overcoming the residues of childhood.

FIFTH LECTURE

LADIES AND GENTLEMEN, - With the discovery of infantile sexuality and the tracing back of neurotic symptoms to erotic instinctual components we have arrived at some unexpected formulas concerning the nature and purposes of neurotic illnesses. We see that human beings fall ill when, as a result of external obstacles or of an internal lack of adaptation, the satisfaction of their erotic needs *in reality* frustrated. We see that they then take flight into *illness* in order that by its help they may find a satisfaction to take the place of what has been frustrated. We recognize that the pathological symptoms constitute a portion of the subject's sexual activity or even the whole of his sexual life, and we find that the withdrawal from reality is the main purpose of the illness but also the main damage caused by it. We suspect that our patients' resistance to recovery is no simple one, but compounded of several motives. Not only does the patient's ego rebel against giving up the repressions by means of which it has risen above its original disposition, but the sexual instincts are unwilling to renounce their substitutive satisfaction so long as it is uncertain whether reality will offer them anything better.

The flight from unsatisfactory reality into what, on account of the biological damage involved, we call illness (though it is never without an immediate yield of pleasure to the patient) takes place along the path of involution, of regression, of a return to earlier phases of sexual life, phases from which at one time satisfaction was not withheld. This regression appears to be a twofold one: a *temporal* one, in so far as the libido, the erotic needs, hark back to stages of development that are earlier in time, and a *formal* one, in that the original and primitive methods of psychical expression are employed in manifesting those needs. Both these kinds of regression, however, lead back to childhood and unite in bringing about an infantile condition of sexual life.

The deeper you penetrate into the pathogenesis of nervous illness, the more you will find revealed the connection between the neuroses and other productions of the human mind, including the most valuable. You will be taught that we humans, with the high standards of our civilization and under the pressure of our internal repressions, find reality unsatisfying quite generally, and for that reason entertain a life of phantasy in which we like to make up for the insufficiencies of reality by the production of wish-fulfilments. These phantasies include a great deal of the true constitutional essence of the subject's personality as well as of those of his impulses which are repressed where reality is concerned. The energetic and successful man is one who succeeds by his efforts in turning his wishful phantasies into reality. Where this fails, as a result of the resistances of the external world and of the subject's own weakness, he begins to turn away from reality and withdraws into his more satisfying world of phantasy, the content of which is transformed into symptoms should he fall ill. In certain favourable circumstances, it still remains possible for him to find another path leading from these phantasies to reality, instead of becoming permanently estranged from it by regressing to infancy. If a person who is at loggerheads with reality possesses an *artistic gift* (a thing that is still a psychological mystery to us), he can transform his phantasies into artistic creations instead of into symptoms. In this manner he can escape the doom of neurosis and by this roundabout path regain his contact with reality. (Cf. Rank, 1907.) If there is persistent rebellion against the real world and if this precious gift is absent or insufficient, it is almost inevitable that the libido, keeping to the sources of the phantasies, will follow the path of regression, and will revive infantile wishes and end in neurosis. To-day neurosis takes the place of the monasteries which used to be the refuge of all whom life had disappointed or who felt too weak to face it.

Let me at this point state the principal finding to which we have been led by the psycho-analytic investigation of neurotics. The neuroses have no psychical content that is peculiar to them and that might not equally be found in healthy people. Or, as Jung has expressed it, neurotics fall ill of the same complexes against which we healthy people struggle as well. Whether that struggle ends in health, in neurosis, or in a countervailing superiority of achievement, depends on *quantitative* considerations, on the relative strength of the conflicting forces.

I have not yet told you, Ladies and Gentlemen, of the most important of the observations which confirm our hypothesis of the sexual instinctual forces operating in neuroses. In every psycho-analytic treatment of a neurotic patient the strange phenomenon that is known as 'transference' makes its appearance. The patient, that is to say, directs towards the physician a degree of affectionate feeling (mingled, often enough, with hostility) which is based on no real relation between them and which - as is shown by every detail of its emergence - can only be traced back to old wishful phantasies of the patient's which have become unconscious. Thus the part of the patient's emotional life which he can no longer recall to memory is re-experienced by him in his relation to the physician; and it is only this re-experiencing in the 'transference' that convinces him of the existence and of the power of these unconscious sexual impulses. His symptoms, to take an analogy from chemistry, are precipitates of earlier experiences in the sphere of love (in the widest sense of the word), and it is only in the raised temperature of his experience of the transference that they can be resolved and reduced to other psychical products. In this reaction the physician, if I may borrow an apt phrase from Ferenczi (1909), plays the part of a catalytic ferment, which temporarily attracts to itself the affects liberated in the process. A study of transference, too, can give you the key to an understanding of hypnotic suggestion, which we employed to begin with as a technical method for investigating the unconscious in our patients. At that time hypnosis was found to be a help therapeutically, but a hindrance to the scientific understanding of the facts; for it cleared away the psychical resistances in a certain area while building them up into an unscalable wall at its frontiers. You must not suppose, moreover, that the phenomenon of transference (of which, unfortunately, I can tell you all too little to-day) is *created* by psycho-analytic influence. Transference arises spontaneously in all human relationships just as it does between the patient and the physician. It is everywhere the true vehicle of therapeutic influence; and the less its presence is suspected, the more powerfully it operates. So psycho-analysis does not create it, but merely reveals it to consciousness and gains control of it in order to guide psychical processes towards the desired goal. I cannot, however, leave the topic of transference without stressing the fact that this phenomenon plays a decisive part in bringing conviction not only to the patient but also to the physician. I know it to be true of all my followers that they were only convinced of the correctness of my assertions on the pathogenesis of the neuroses by their experiences with transference; and I can very well understand that such certainty of judgement cannot be attained before one has carried out psycho-analyses and has oneself observed the workings of transference.

Ladies and Gentlemen, from the intellectual point of view we must, I think, take into account two special obstacles to recognizing psycho-analytic trains of thought. In the first place, people are unaccustomed to reckoning with a strict and universal application of determinism to mental life; and in the second place, they are ignorant of the peculiarities which distinguish unconscious mental processes from the conscious ones that are familiar to us. One of the most widespread resistances to psycho-analytic work, in the sick and healthy alike, can be traced to the second of these two factors. People are afraid of doing harm by psycho-analysis; they are afraid of bringing the repressed sexual instincts into the patient's consciousness, as though that involved a danger of their overwhelming his higher ethical trends and of their robbing him of his cultural acquisitions. People notice that the patient has sore spots in his mind, but shrink from touching them for fear of increasing his sufferings. We can accept this analogy. It is no doubt kinder not to touch diseased spots if it can do nothing else but cause pain. But, as we know, a surgeon does not refrain from examining and handling a focus of disease, if he is intending to take active measures which he believes will lead to a permanent cure. No one thinks of blaming him for the inevitable suffering caused by the examination or for the reactions to the operation, if only it gains its end and the patient achieves a lasting recovery as a result of the temporary worsening of his state. The case is similar with psycho-analysis. It may make the same claims as surgery: the increase in suffering which it causes the patient during treatment is incomparably less than what a surgeon causes, and is quite negligible in proportion to the severity of the underlying ailment. On the other hand, the final outcome that is so much dreaded - the destruction of the patient's cultural character by the instincts which have been set free from repression - is totally impossible. For alarm on this score takes no account of what our experiences have taught us with certainty - namely that the mental and somatic power of a wishful impulse, when once its repression has failed, is far stronger if it is unconscious than if it is conscious; so that to make it conscious can only be to weaken it. An unconscious wish cannot be influenced and it is independent of any contrary tendencies, whereas a conscious one is inhibited by whatever else is conscious and opposed to it. Thus the work of psycho-analysis puts itself at the orders of precisely the highest and most valuable cultural trends, as a better substitute for the unsuccessful repression.

What, then, becomes of the unconscious wishes which have been set free by psycho-analysis? Along what paths do we succeed in making them harmless to the subject's life? There are several such paths. The most frequent outcome is that, while the work is actually going on, these wishes are destroyed by the rational mental activity of the better impulses that are opposed to them. *Repression* is replaced by a *condemning judgement* carried out along the best lines. That is possible because what we have to get rid of is to a great extent only the consequences arising from earlier stages of the ego's development. The subject only succeeded in the past in repressing the unserviceable instinct because he himself was at that time still imperfectly organized and feeble. In his present-day maturity and strength, he will perhaps be able to master what is hostile to him with complete success.

A second outcome of the work of psycho-analysis is that it then becomes possible for the unconscious instincts revealed by it to be employed for the useful purposes which they would have found earlier if development had not been interrupted. For the extirpation of the infantile wishful impulses is by no means the ideal aim of development. Owing to their repressions, neurotics have sacrificed many sources of mental energy whose contributions would have been of great value in the formation of their character and in their activity in life. We know of a far more expedient process of development, called '*sublimation*', in which the energy of the infantile wishful impulses is not cut off but remains ready for use - the unserviceable aim of the various impulses being replaced by one that is higher, and perhaps no longer sexual. It happens to be precisely the components of the *sexual* instinct that are specially marked by a capacity of this kind for sublimation, for exchanging their sexual aim for another one which is comparatively remote and socially valuable. It is probable that we owe our highest cultural successes to the contributions of energy made in this way to our mental functions. Premature repression makes the sublimation of the repressed instinct impossible; when the repression is lifted, the path to sublimation becomes free once more.

We must not omit to consider the third of the possible outcomes of the work of psycho-analysis. A certain portion of the repressed libidinal impulses has a claim to direct satisfaction and ought to find it in life. Our civilized standards make life too difficult for the majority of human organizations. Those standards consequently encourage the retreat from reality and the generating of neuroses, without achieving any surplus of cultural gain by this excess of sexual repression. We ought not to exalt ourselves so high as completely to neglect what was originally animal in our nature. Nor should we forget that the satisfaction of the individual's happiness cannot be erased from among the aims of our civilization. The plasticity of the components of sexuality, shown by their capacity for sublimation, may indeed offer a great temptation to strive for still greater cultural achievements by still further sublimation. But, just as we do not count on our machines converting more than a certain fraction of the heat consumed into useful mechanical work, we ought not to seek to alienate the whole amount of the energy of the sexual instinct from its proper ends. We cannot succeed in doing so; and if the restriction upon sexuality were to be carried too far it would inevitably bring with it all the evils of soil-exhaustion.

It may be that you for your part will regard the warning with which I close as an exaggeration. I shall only venture on an indirect picture of my conviction by telling you an old story and leaving you to make what use you like of it. German literature is familiar with a little town called Schilda, to whose inhabitants clever tricks of every possible sort are attributed. The citizens of Schilda, so we are told, possessed a horse with whose feats of strength they were highly pleased and against which they had only one objection - that it consumed such a large quantity of expensive oats. They determined to break it of this bad habit very gently by reducing its ration by a few stalks every day, till they had accustomed it to complete abstinence. For a time things went excellently: the horse was weaned to the point of eating only one stalk a day, and on the succeeding day it was at length to work without any oats at all. On the morning of that day the spiteful animal was found dead; and the citizens of Schilda could not make out what it had died of.

We should be inclined to think that the horse was starved and that no work at all could be expected of an animal without a certain modicum of oats.

I must thank you for your invitation and for the attention with which you have listened to me.

Printed in Great Britain
by Amazon

18027085R00051